The Art of Apple Preserves

A Comprehensive Apple Jam Cookbook

THE ART OF APPLE PRESERVES

First edition. January 27, 2024.

ISBN: 979-8223184737

Written by Jose Maria.

Table of Contents

The Art of Apple Preserves 1

Chapter (1) Getting Started 4

Chapter (2) Basic Apple Jam Recipes 6

Chapter (3) Creative Apple Jam Variations 10

Chapter (4) Sugar-Free and Low-Sugar Options 14

Chapter (5) Seasonal Apple Jam Delights 16

Chapter (6) Savory Apple Jam Applications 19

Chapter (7) Gift Ideas and Packaging 22

Chapter (8) Troubleshooting and FAQs 24

Chapter (9) International Apple Jam Flavors 27

Chapter (10) Health-Conscious Apple Jams 30

Chapter (11) Family-Friendly Apple Jam Creations 33

Chapter (12) No-Cook Apple Jam Recipes 35

Chapter (13) Apple Jam Cocktails and Mocktails 37

Chapter (14) Apple Jam-Inspired Desserts 39

Chapter (15) Homestead Orchard Tales 42

Chapter (16) DIY Apple Jam Wedding Favors 44

Chapter (16) Apple Jam and Cheese Pairing Guide 46

Chapter (17) Apple Jam for Wellness 48

Chapter (18) Preserving Memories: Scrapbooking with Apple Jam Labels 50

Chapter (19) Apple Jam and Cultural Festivals 53

Chapter (20) Vegan Apple Jam Options 56

Chapter (21) Festive Holiday Extravaganza: Spiced Apple Jam Gift Collection 59

Chapter (22) Culinary Adventures with Apple Jam: Cooking Classes and Workshops 62

Chapter (23) The Science of Jam: Understanding Pectin and Gel Points 65

Jose Maria

❖ Introduction

A. Welcome to the World of Apple Jams

Welcome to a delightful journey into the world of apple jams, where the sweet aroma of simmering fruit fills your kitchen, and the satisfaction of crafting your own preserves warms your heart. Whether you're a seasoned jam enthusiast or a novice in the world of homemade preserves, this comprehensive cookbook is your guide to mastering the art of apple jams.

Unlock the secrets to creating luscious spreads that capture the essence of fresh, juicy apples in every spoonful. From classic recipes to innovative variations, you'll embark on a culinary adventure that transforms ordinary apples into extraordinary jams.

B. Brief History of Apple Preserves

Delve into the rich history of apple preserves, a tradition that spans centuries and continents. Apples, abundant in various regions, have been cherished for their versatility in culinary applications. The practice of preserving apples dates back to ancient times when civilizations discovered the art of capturing the harvest's bounty for prolonged enjoyment.

Explore how apple jams evolved over the years, adapting to different cultures and tastes. From medieval kitchens to colonial pantries, apples have played a central role in the world of preserves, and this cookbook invites you to be part of this enduring legacy.

C. Benefits of Making Your Own Apple Jam

Discover the numerous benefits of crafting your own apple jams at home. Beyond the irresistible flavors and aromas, homemade preserves offer a host of advantages. You have control over the quality of ingredients, enabling you to create healthier, preservative-free options.

Furthermore, making your own apple jam allows you to tailor recipes to your taste preferences. Experiment with various apple varieties, sweeteners, and flavor infusions to create jams that suit your palate perfectly. Engage in a fulfilling, hands-on experience that not only yields delicious results but also fosters a connection to the traditions of preserving seasonal abundance.

As we embark on this apple jam-making journey together, let the joy of crafting your own preserves inspire you to create moments of sweetness and connection in your kitchen and beyond.

Chapter (1) Getting Started

A. Essential Ingredients

Types of Apples for Jam

Selecting the right apples is crucial for a flavorful jam. Opt for a mix of sweet and tart varieties, such as Honeycrisp, Granny Smith, or a combination of both. Experiment with local or seasonal apples for unique flavor profiles.

Sweeteners and Sugar Ratios

Choose high-quality sweeteners to complement the natural sweetness of the apples. Granulated sugar is a classic choice, but you can also explore alternatives like honey, maple syrup, or agave nectar for distinct flavors. Balancing the sweetness is key, and a common ratio is about 4 cups of chopped apples to 3 cups of sugar.

Pectin Options

Pectin is a natural thickening agent found in fruits. While some apples naturally contain pectin, you may choose to add commercial pectin for a firmer jam texture. Follow package instructions for the appropriate quantity based on your recipe.

B. Necessary Equipment

Canning Jars and Lids

Use clean, sterilized glass jars with tight-fitting lids to ensure the longevity of your jams. Choose jars of various sizes depending on your preferences and the intended use of the jam. Ensure the lids are free from dents or defects for a proper seal during the canning process.

Cooking Utensils

Gather essential kitchen tools, including a large, heavy-bottomed pot for cooking the jam, a ladle for filling jars, a wide-mouth funnel for easy pouring, and a wooden spoon for stirring. Ensure all utensils are clean and in good condition.

Water Bath Canning Basics

Familiarize yourself with water bath canning, a method that preserves jams by immersing sealed jars in boiling water. Equip yourself with a canning pot, a jar lifter for safe removal of hot jars, and a canning rack to keep jars elevated during the water bath.

As you embark on your jam-making adventure, having the right ingredients and equipment sets the foundation for successful and enjoyable preserves. Prepare your kitchen with care, and let the art of apple jam-making unfold.

Chapter (2) Basic Apple Jam Recipes

A. Classic Apple Jam

Ingredients:

- 4 cups finely chopped mixed apples (Honeycrisp, Granny Smith)
- 3 cups granulated sugar
- 1 lemon (juiced)
- 1 teaspoon natural pectin (optional for firmer texture)

Instructions:

1. In a large pot, combine chopped apples, sugar, and lemon juice. Let it sit for 15-20 minutes to allow the sugar to draw out the juices.
2. Over medium heat, bring the mixture to a boil, stirring frequently. Skim off any foam that rises to the surface.
3. Reduce heat to a simmer and cook until the jam reaches the desired consistency, typically around 20-30 minutes. If using pectin, add it according to package instructions.
4. Perform a spoon or plate test to check the jam's thickness. Once ready, remove from heat.
5. Ladle the hot jam into sterilized jars, leaving about 1/4-inch headspace. Wipe the jar rims, place lids, and tighten the bands until snug.
6. Process the jars in a boiling water bath for 10 minutes. Allow jars to cool, and ensure lids have sealed properly before storing.

B. Cinnamon-Spiced Apple Jam

Ingredients:

- 4 cups finely chopped mixed apples (Gala, Fuji)
- 2 ½ cups granulated sugar
- 1 lemon (juiced)
- 1 teaspoon ground cinnamon
- 1/2 teaspoon ground nutmeg
- 1 teaspoon natural pectin (optional)

Instructions:

1. Follow the same instructions as the Classic Apple Jam, adding ground cinnamon and nutmeg when combining apples, sugar, and lemon juice.
2. Continue with the cooking process, adjusting the heat to low-medium once the mixture starts boiling.
3. Stir in the optional pectin if a firmer texture is desired.
4. Complete the canning process as outlined in the Classic Apple Jam recipe.

C. Vanilla Bean Apple Jam
Ingredients:

- 4 cups finely chopped mixed apples (Braeburn, Pink Lady)
- 3 cups granulated sugar
- 1 lemon (juiced)
- 1 vanilla bean (seeds scraped)
- 1 teaspoon natural pectin (optional)

Instructions:

1. Follow the same instructions as the Classic Apple Jam, adding the vanilla bean seeds when combining apples, sugar, and lemon juice.
2. Continue with the cooking process, ensuring the vanilla infuses into the jam.

3. Stir in the optional pectin if a firmer texture is desired.
4. Complete the canning process as outlined in the Classic Apple Jam recipe.

D. Honey-Apple Jam
Ingredients:

- 4 cups finely chopped mixed apples (Golden Delicious, McIntosh)
- 2 ½ cups honey
- 1 lemon (juiced)
- 1 teaspoon natural pectin (optional)

Instructions:

1. In a large pot, combine chopped apples, honey, and lemon juice. Allow it to sit for 15-20 minutes.
2. Bring the mixture to a gentle boil over medium heat, stirring frequently.
3. Simmer until the jam thickens, typically around 25-35 minutes. Stir in the optional pectin if desired.
4. Perform a spoon or plate test, and once the jam has reached the desired consistency, proceed to jar and process as outlined in the Classic Apple Jam recipe.

E. Ginger-Infused Apple Jam
Ingredients:

- 4 cups finely chopped mixed apples (Jonagold, Empire)
- 3 cups granulated sugar
- 1 lemon (juiced)
- 1 tablespoon fresh ginger (grated)
- 1 teaspoon natural pectin (optional)

Instructions:

1. Follow the same instructions as the Classic Apple Jam, adding the grated ginger when combining apples, sugar, and lemon juice.
2. Continue with the cooking process, ensuring the ginger infuses into the jam.
3. Stir in the optional pectin if a firmer texture is desired.
4. Complete the canning process as outlined in the Classic Apple Jam recipe.
5. Enjoy the delightful array of basic apple jam recipes, each offering a unique twist on traditional flavors.

Chapter (3) Creative Apple Jam Variations

A. Apple and Berry Fusion Jam
Ingredients:

- 3 cups finely chopped mixed apples (Pink Lady, Braeburn)
- 1 cup mixed berries (strawberries, blueberries, raspberries)
- 3 cups granulated sugar
- 1 lemon (juiced)
- 1 teaspoon natural pectin (optional)

Instructions:

1. Combine chopped apples, mixed berries, sugar, and lemon juice in a large pot.
2. Let the mixture sit for 15-20 minutes to allow the sugar to draw out juices.
3. Bring the mixture to a boil over medium heat, stirring frequently.
4. Reduce heat to a simmer and cook until the jam reaches the desired consistency, approximately 20-30 minutes.
5. Stir in the optional pectin if a firmer texture is desired.
6. Jar and process as outlined in the Classic Apple Jam recipe.

B. Apple-Rosemary Jam
Ingredients:

- 4 cups finely chopped mixed apples (Gravenstein, Jonagold)
- 3 cups granulated sugar
- 1 lemon (juiced)
- 2 tablespoons fresh rosemary (finely chopped)
- 1 teaspoon natural pectin (optional)

Instructions:

1. Combine chopped apples, sugar, lemon juice, and fresh rosemary in a large pot.
2. Let the mixture sit for 15-20 minutes.
3. Bring the mixture to a boil over medium heat, stirring frequently.
4. Reduce heat to a simmer and cook until the jam reaches the desired consistency, about 20-30 minutes.
5. Stir in the optional pectin if a firmer texture is desired.
6. Jar and process as outlined in the Classic Apple Jam recipe.

C. Maple-Pecan Apple Jam
Ingredients:

- 4 cups finely chopped mixed apples (Cortland, Empire)
- 2 ½ cups granulated sugar
- 1 lemon (juiced)
- 1/2 cup pure maple syrup
- 1/2 cup chopped pecans
- 1 teaspoon natural pectin (optional)

Instructions:

1. Combine chopped apples, sugar, lemon juice, maple syrup, and chopped pecans in a large pot.
2. Let the mixture sit for 15-20 minutes.
3. Bring the mixture to a boil over medium heat, stirring frequently.
4. Reduce heat to a simmer and cook until the jam reaches the desired consistency, around 25-35 minutes.
5. Stir in the optional pectin if a firmer texture is desired.
6. Jar and process as outlined in the Classic Apple Jam recipe.

D. Bourbon-Infused Apple Jam
Ingredients:

- 4 cups finely chopped mixed apples (Braeburn, Fuji)
- 3 cups granulated sugar
- 1 lemon (juiced)
- 1/2 cup bourbon
- 1 teaspoon natural pectin (optional)

Instructions:

1. Combine chopped apples, sugar, lemon juice, and bourbon in a large pot.
2. Let the mixture sit for 15-20 minutes.
3. Bring the mixture to a boil over medium heat, stirring frequently.
4. Reduce heat to a simmer and cook until the jam reaches the desired consistency, approximately 20-30 minutes.
5. Stir in the optional pectin if a firmer texture is desired.
6. Jar and process as outlined in the Classic Apple Jam recipe.

E. Chai-Spiced Apple Jam
Ingredients:

- 4 cups finely chopped mixed apples (Honeycrisp, Gala)
- 3 cups granulated sugar
- 1 lemon (juiced)
- 1 tablespoon chai spice blend (cinnamon, cardamom, ginger, cloves)
- 1 teaspoon natural pectin (optional)

Instructions:

1. Combine chopped apples, sugar, lemon juice, and chai spice blend in a large pot.
2. Let the mixture sit for 15-20 minutes.
3. Bring the mixture to a boil over medium heat, stirring frequently.
4. Reduce heat to a simmer and cook until the jam reaches the desired consistency, approximately 20-30 minutes.
5. Stir in the optional pectin if a firmer texture is desired.
6. Jar and process as outlined in the Classic Apple Jam recipe.

Indulge in the diverse and enticing flavors of these creative apple jam variations. Each recipe promises a delightful fusion of tastes that will elevate your homemade jam experience.

Chapter (4) Sugar-Free and Low-Sugar Options

A. Stevia-Sweetened Apple Jam
   Ingredients:

- 4 cups finely chopped mixed apples (Granny Smith, Pink Lady)
- 1 cup granulated stevia (or to taste)
- 1 lemon (juiced)
- 1 teaspoon natural pectin (optional)

Instructions:

1. Combine chopped apples, stevia, and lemon juice in a large pot.
2. Let the mixture sit for 15-20 minutes to allow the stevia to dissolve.
3. Bring the mixture to a boil over medium heat, stirring frequently.
4. Reduce heat to a simmer and cook until the jam reaches the desired consistency, around 20-30 minutes.
5. Stir in the optional pectin if a firmer texture is desired.
6. Jar and process as outlined in the Classic Apple Jam recipe.

B. Agave Nectar Apple Jam
Ingredients:

- 4 cups finely chopped mixed apples (Honeycrisp, Fuji)
- 1 ½ cups agave nectar
- 1 lemon (juiced)
- 1 teaspoon natural pectin (optional)

Instructions:

1. Combine chopped apples, agave nectar, and lemon juice in a large pot.
2. Let the mixture sit for 15-20 minutes.
3. Bring the mixture to a boil over medium heat, stirring frequently.
4. Reduce heat to a simmer and cook until the jam reaches the desired consistency, typically around 20-30 minutes.
5. Stir in the optional pectin if a firmer texture is desired.
6. Jar and process as outlined in the Classic Apple Jam recipe.

C. Reduced-Sugar Apple Jam
Ingredients:

- 4 cups finely chopped mixed apples (Gala, McIntosh)
- 2 cups granulated sugar
- 1 lemon (juiced)
- 1 teaspoon natural pectin (optional)

Instructions:

1. Combine chopped apples, sugar, and lemon juice in a large pot.
2. Let the mixture sit for 15-20 minutes to draw out juices.
3. Bring the mixture to a boil over medium heat, stirring frequently.
4. Reduce heat to a simmer and cook until the jam reaches the desired consistency, approximately 20-30 minutes.
5. Stir in the optional pectin if a firmer texture is desired.
6. Jar and process as outlined in the Classic Apple Jam recipe.

Explore the world of sugar-free and low-sugar options with these delicious apple jam recipes. Whether you prefer the natural sweetness of stevia, the unique flavor of agave nectar, or a reduced-sugar version, these recipes offer a delightful twist on traditional jams.

Chapter (5) Seasonal Apple Jam Delights

A. Spiced Autumn Apple Jam
  Ingredients:

- 4 cups finely chopped mixed apples (Jonagold, Honeycrisp)
- 3 cups brown sugar
- 1 lemon (juiced)
- 1 teaspoon ground cinnamon
- 1/2 teaspoon ground nutmeg
- 1/4 teaspoon ground cloves
- 1 teaspoon natural pectin (optional)

Instructions:

1. Combine chopped apples, brown sugar, lemon juice, and spices in a large pot.
2. Let the mixture sit for 15-20 minutes to allow the sugar to draw out juices.
3. Bring the mixture to a boil over medium heat, stirring frequently.
4. Reduce heat to a simmer and cook until the jam reaches the desired consistency, approximately 25-35 minutes.
5. Stir in the optional pectin if a firmer texture is desired.
6. Jar and process as outlined in the Classic Apple Jam recipe.

B. Cranberry-Apple Jam for the Holidays
Ingredients:

- 3 cups finely chopped mixed apples (Crispin, Gala)
- 1 cup fresh or frozen cranberries
- 3 cups granulated sugar
- 1 orange (zested and juiced)

- 1 teaspoon natural pectin (optional)

Instructions:

1. Combine chopped apples, cranberries, sugar, orange zest, and orange juice in a large pot.
2. Let the mixture sit for 15-20 minutes.
3. Bring the mixture to a boil over medium heat, stirring frequently.
4. Reduce heat to a simmer and cook until the jam reaches the desired consistency, approximately 20-30 minutes.
5. Stir in the optional pectin if a firmer texture is desired.
6. Jar and process as outlined in the Classic Apple Jam recipe.

C. Fresh Mint and Apple Jam for Spring
Ingredients:

- 4 cups finely chopped mixed apples (Ginger Gold, Pink Lady)
- 3 cups granulated sugar
- 1 lemon (juiced)
- 1/2 cup fresh mint leaves (chopped)
- 1 teaspoon natural pectin (optional)

Instructions:

1. Combine chopped apples, sugar, lemon juice, and fresh mint in a large pot.
2. Let the mixture sit for 15-20 minutes.
3. Bring the mixture to a boil over medium heat, stirring frequently.
4. Reduce heat to a simmer and cook until the jam reaches the desired consistency, around 20-30 minutes.
5. Stir in the optional pectin if a firmer texture is desired.
6. Jar and process as outlined in the Classic Apple Jam recipe.

Celebrate the changing seasons with these delightful apple jam variations. Whether you're capturing the warmth of autumn spices, creating a festive cranberry-apple blend for the holidays, or infusing the freshness of mint for spring, these recipes are sure to brighten your kitchen and your taste buds.

Chapter (6) Savory Apple Jam Applications

A. Apple and Onion Jam for Cheese Boards
Ingredients:

- 4 cups finely chopped mixed apples (Golden Delicious, McIntosh)
- 2 cups red onions (finely chopped)
- 1 ½ cups brown sugar
- 1 cup apple cider vinegar
- 1 teaspoon mustard seeds
- 1 teaspoon natural pectin (optional)

Instructions:

1. In a large pot, combine chopped apples, red onions, brown sugar, apple cider vinegar, and mustard seeds.
2. Let the mixture sit for 15-20 minutes.
3. Bring the mixture to a boil over medium heat, stirring frequently.
4. Reduce heat to a simmer and cook until the jam reaches the desired consistency, approximately 30-40 minutes.
5. Stir in the optional pectin if a firmer texture is desired.
6. Jar and process as outlined in the Classic Apple Jam recipe.

B. Bacon-Apple Jam for Savory Dishes
Ingredients:

- 4 cups finely chopped mixed apples (Braeburn, Granny Smith)
- 1 cup cooked bacon (crumbled)
- 2 cups granulated sugar
- 1 lemon (juiced)

- 1 teaspoon smoked paprika
- 1 teaspoon natural pectin (optional)

Instructions:

1. Combine chopped apples, crumbled bacon, sugar, lemon juice, and smoked paprika in a large pot.
2. Let the mixture sit for 15-20 minutes.
3. Bring the mixture to a boil over medium heat, stirring frequently.
4. Reduce heat to a simmer and cook until the jam reaches the desired consistency, around 25-35 minutes.
5. Stir in the optional pectin if a firmer texture is desired.
6. Jar and process as outlined in the Classic Apple Jam recipe.

C. Apple Balsamic Reduction Jam
Ingredients:

- 4 cups finely chopped mixed apples (Fuji, Cortland)
- 1 cup balsamic vinegar
- 1 cup granulated sugar
- 1 teaspoon dried thyme
- 1 teaspoon natural pectin (optional)

Instructions:

1. Combine chopped apples, balsamic vinegar, sugar, and dried thyme in a large pot.
2. Let the mixture sit for 15-20 minutes.
3. Bring the mixture to a boil over medium heat, stirring frequently.
4. Reduce heat to a simmer and cook until the jam reaches the desired consistency, approximately 25-35 minutes.
5. Stir in the optional pectin if a firmer texture is desired.

6. Jar and process as outlined in the Classic Apple Jam recipe.

Explore the savory side of apple jams with these delightful recipes. Whether you're enhancing cheese boards with a sweet and tangy apple and onion jam, adding a savory twist to dishes with bacon-apple jam, or drizzling a balsamic reduction jam for a gourmet touch, these savory applications are sure to elevate your culinary creations.

Chapter (7) Gift Ideas and Packaging

A. Creative Jar Labeling

Personalize your homemade apple jams with creative and eye-catching labels. Here's a simple guide:

Materials:

- Printable labels or plain paper
- Colored markers or pens
- Decorative stickers or washi tape
- Clear adhesive tape

Instructions:

1. Print or cut labels to fit the jar lids or sides.
2. Use colored markers or pens to write the jam flavor, date, and any special notes.
3. Add decorative stickers or washi tape to enhance the visual appeal.
4. Secure the label to the jar using clear adhesive tape.
5. Get creative with your labeling, matching colors and themes to the jam's flavor or the occasion. This personal touch adds a special flair to your homemade gifts.

B. DIY Gift Basket Ideas

Create charming gift baskets featuring your homemade apple jams. Here are three thematic ideas:

1. Breakfast Delight Basket:

Include a jar of Vanilla Bean Apple Jam and a selection of gourmet breakfast items like pancake mix, artisanal syrups, and a stylish breakfast mug.

2. Cheese Lover's Basket:

Pair a jar of Apple and Onion Jam with a variety of artisan cheeses, crackers, and a cheese board. Add a small cheese knife for an elegant touch.

3. Relaxation Basket:

Combine a jar of Chai-Spiced Apple Jam with a selection of soothing teas, honey sticks, and a cozy blanket or tea infuser. Perfect for a relaxing evening.

C. Tips for Storing and Gifting Apple Jam

Storing:

- Store jars in a cool, dark place away from direct sunlight.
- Ensure lids are tightly sealed to preserve freshness.
- Use within a year for optimal flavor, although most jams can last longer.

Gifting:

- Attach a personalized label with a brief description of the jam and serving suggestions.
- Consider including a small recipe card using the jam in a creative dish.
- Use decorative ribbons or twine to tie a tag around the jar neck for an added festive touch.

By presenting your homemade apple jams thoughtfully, you turn a simple jar into a cherished gift. Whether labeling, creating themed gift baskets, or offering storage tips, these ideas ensure your jams are both visually appealing and delightful to receive.

Chapter (8) Troubleshooting and FAQs

A. Common Issues in Jam-Making

1. Jam is Too Runny:

Possible Causes:

- Undercooking or insufficient pectin.
- Incorrect sugar-to-fruit ratio.

Solution:

- Return the jam to the heat and cook longer, testing for thickness using a spoon or plate test.
- Ensure the correct sugar-to-fruit ratio or consider adding commercial pectin.

2. Jam is Too Thick:

Possible Causes:

- Overcooking or using too much pectin.
- High-pectin apples combined with commercial pectin.

Solution:

- Add additional liquid (water, fruit juice) to reach the desired consistency.
- Adjust the pectin quantity in future batches.

3. Jam Has Crystalized Sugar:

Possible Causes:

- Sugar not fully dissolved during cooking.
- Jam cooled too quickly.

Solution:

- Ensure sugar is fully dissolved before bringing the mixture to a boil.
- Stir the jam gently while cooling to prevent rapid crystallization.

4. Jars Didn't Seal Properly:
Possible Causes:

- Jars or lids weren't properly sterilized.
- Incorrect headspace when filling jars.

Solution:

- Re-process the jars with new lids, ensuring proper sterilization.
- Leave the recommended headspace to allow for proper sealing.

B. Frequently Asked Questions
1. Can I Use Frozen Fruit?
Yes, frozen fruit can be used. Thaw it first and drain excess liquid before adding it to the recipe.
2. Can I Reduce the Sugar Content?
Yes, but it may affect the jam's consistency and shelf life. Use low-sugar or no-sugar pectin if reducing sugar.
3. How Do I Know When the Jam is Ready?
Perform a spoon or plate test. Place a small amount on a chilled plate; if it wrinkles when touched, it's ready.
4. Can I Double or Halve the Recipes?
Yes, but maintain the correct proportions of fruit, sugar, and pectin. Adjust cooking times accordingly.
5. Why Did My Jam Change Color?
Natural variations can occur due to apple varieties and cooking times. Adding lemon juice helps preserve the color.

6. Can I Reuse Jars and Lids?

Jars can be reused, but always use new lids to ensure a proper seal.

Addressing these common issues and providing answers to frequently asked questions will help ensure a successful and enjoyable experience for anyone venturing into the world of apple jam-making.

Chapter (9) International Apple Jam Flavors

A. French Apple Calvados Jam
Ingredients:

- 4 cups finely chopped mixed apples (Gravenstein, Pink Lady)
- 2 cups granulated sugar
- 1 lemon (juiced)
- 1/2 cup Calvados (apple brandy)
- 1 teaspoon natural pectin (optional)

Instructions:

1. Combine chopped apples, sugar, lemon juice, and Calvados in a large pot.
2. Let the mixture sit for 15-20 minutes.
3. Bring the mixture to a boil over medium heat, stirring frequently.
4. Reduce heat to a simmer and cook until the jam reaches the desired consistency, around 25-35 minutes.
5. Stir in the optional pectin if a firmer texture is desired.
6. Jar and process as outlined in the Classic Apple Jam recipe.

B. Italian Amaretto-Infused Apple Jam
Ingredients:

- 4 cups finely chopped mixed apples (Braeburn, Fuji)
- 2 ½ cups granulated sugar
- 1 lemon (juiced)
- 1/2 cup Amaretto liqueur
- 1/2 cup sliced almonds
- 1 teaspoon natural pectin (optional)

Instructions:

1. Combine chopped apples, sugar, lemon juice, Amaretto, and sliced almonds in a large pot.
2. Let the mixture sit for 15-20 minutes.
3. Bring the mixture to a boil over medium heat, stirring frequently.
4. Reduce heat to a simmer and cook until the jam reaches the desired consistency, approximately 20-30 minutes.
5. Stir in the optional pectin if a firmer texture is desired.
6. Jar and process as outlined in the Classic Apple Jam recipe.

C. Japanese Matcha Green Tea Apple Jam
Ingredients:

- 4 cups finely chopped mixed apples (Honeycrisp, Gala)
- 3 cups granulated sugar
- 1 lemon (juiced)
- 2 tablespoons Matcha green tea powder
- 1 teaspoon natural pectin (optional)

Instructions:

1. Combine chopped apples, sugar, lemon juice, and Matcha green tea powder in a large pot.
2. Let the mixture sit for 15-20 minutes.
3. Bring the mixture to a boil over medium heat, stirring frequently.
4. Reduce heat to a simmer and cook until the jam reaches the desired consistency, around 20-30 minutes.
5. Stir in the optional pectin if a firmer texture is desired.
6. Jar and process as outlined in the Classic Apple Jam recipe.

Indulge in the international flavors of these unique apple jam recipes. Whether you're savoring the French elegance of Calvados, enjoying the Italian warmth of Amaretto, or embracing the Japanese essence of Matcha, these international variations add a global touch to your homemade jam collection.

Chapter (10) Health-Conscious Apple Jams

A. Chia Seed and Apple Jam
Ingredients:

- 4 cups finely chopped mixed apples (Gala, Fuji)
- 2 ½ cups honey or maple syrup
- 1 lemon (juiced)
- 3 tablespoons chia seeds
- 1 teaspoon natural pectin (optional)

Instructions:

1. In a large pot, combine chopped apples, honey or maple syrup, and lemon juice.
2. Let the mixture sit for 15-20 minutes.
3. Bring the mixture to a boil over medium heat, stirring frequently.
4. Reduce heat to a simmer and cook until the jam reaches the desired consistency, around 25-35 minutes.
5. Stir in the chia seeds and optional pectin. Continue simmering for an additional 5 minutes.
6. Jar and process as outlined in the Classic Apple Jam recipe.

B. Turmeric and Ginger Apple Jam
Ingredients:

- 4 cups finely chopped mixed apples (Honeycrisp, Pink Lady)
- 2 cups coconut sugar
- 1 lemon (juiced)
- 1 tablespoon fresh ginger (grated)
- 1 teaspoon ground turmeric

- 1 teaspoon natural pectin (optional)

Instructions:

1. Combine chopped apples, coconut sugar, lemon juice, grated ginger, and ground turmeric in a large pot.
2. Let the mixture sit for 15-20 minutes.
3. Bring the mixture to a boil over medium heat, stirring frequently.
4. Reduce heat to a simmer and cook until the jam reaches the desired consistency, approximately 25-35 minutes.
5. Stir in the optional pectin if a firmer texture is desired.
6. Jar and process as outlined in the Classic Apple Jam recipe.

C. Antioxidant-Packed Apple Blueberry Jam

Ingredients:

- 3 cups finely chopped mixed apples (Crispin, Empire)
- 1 cup fresh or frozen blueberries
- 2 ½ cups agave nectar
- 1 lemon (juiced)
- 1 teaspoon natural pectin (optional)

Instructions:

1. Combine chopped apples, blueberries, agave nectar, and lemon juice in a large pot.
2. Let the mixture sit for 15-20 minutes.
3. Bring the mixture to a boil over medium heat, stirring frequently.
4. Reduce heat to a simmer and cook until the jam reaches the desired consistency, around 20-30 minutes.
5. Stir in the optional pectin if a firmer texture is desired.
6. Jar and process as outlined in the Classic Apple Jam recipe.

Embrace health-conscious choices with these nutritious apple jam recipes. Whether incorporating chia seeds for added omega-3s, infusing the anti-inflammatory properties of turmeric and ginger, or enjoying the antioxidant benefits of blueberries, these recipes prioritize both flavor and well-being.

Chapter (11) Family-Friendly Apple Jam Creations

A. Peanut Butter and Apple Jam Sandwich
Ingredients:

- Whole-grain bread slices
- Peanut butter
- Apple jam (Classic Apple Jam or preferred variation)

Instructions:

1. Spread peanut butter on one side of a whole-grain bread slice.
2. On another slice, spread a generous layer of apple jam.
3. Press the slices together to create a delicious and family-friendly Peanut Butter and Apple Jam Sandwich.

B. Apple Jam-filled Muffins
Ingredients:

- 2 cups all-purpose flour
- 1/2 cup sugar
- 1 tablespoon baking powder
- 1/2 teaspoon salt
- 1 cup milk
- 1/4 cup vegetable oil
- 1 large egg
- 1 teaspoon vanilla extract
- Apple jam (any variation)

Instructions:

1. Preheat the oven to 375°F (190°C) and line a muffin tin with

paper liners.

2. In a large bowl, whisk together the flour, sugar, baking powder, and salt.
3. In another bowl, whisk together the milk, vegetable oil, egg, and vanilla extract.
4. Pour the wet ingredients into the dry ingredients and stir until just combined.
5. Spoon the batter into the muffin cups, filling each about halfway.
6. Add a small spoonful of apple jam to the center of each muffin.
7. Top with more batter until the jam is covered.
8. Bake for 18-20 minutes or until a toothpick inserted into the center comes out clean.
9. Allow the muffins to cool before serving.

C. Kid-Friendly Apple Jam Popsicles
Ingredients:

- 2 cups apple juice
- Apple jam (any variation)

Instructions:

1. Mix apple juice with apple jam in a bowl, ensuring the jam is well dissolved.
2. Pour the mixture into popsicle molds.
3. Freeze for at least 4-6 hours or until fully set.
4. Enjoy these refreshing Kid-Friendly Apple Jam Popsicles on a hot day.

These family-friendly apple jam creations are sure to be a hit with kids and adults alike. Whether it's a classic sandwich, muffins with a fruity surprise, or a refreshing popsicle treat, these recipes are perfect for sharing moments of joy with loved ones.

Chapter (12) No-Cook Apple Jam Recipes

A. Quick and Easy Apple Jam
Ingredients:

- 4 cups finely chopped mixed apples (Your choice of sweet varieties)
- 2 cups granulated sugar
- 1 lemon (juiced)
- 1 tablespoon chia seeds

Instructions:

1. In a large bowl, combine chopped apples, sugar, and lemon juice.
2. Let the mixture sit for at least 30 minutes or until the sugar is dissolved.
3. Stir in chia seeds.
4. Transfer the mixture to jars and refrigerate for at least 4 hours or overnight.
5. The chia seeds will thicken the jam. Stir before serving.

B. Raw Apple Jam with Nuts and Seeds
Ingredients:

1. 3 cups finely chopped mixed apples (Honeycrisp, Gala)
2. 1 cup mixed nuts (almonds, walnuts, or your choice)
3. 1/2 cup mixed seeds (sunflower seeds, chia seeds)
4. 1/4 cup honey or maple syrup
5. 1 lemon (juiced)

Instructions:

1. In a food processor, combine chopped apples, mixed nuts,

mixed seeds, honey or maple syrup, and lemon juice.

2. Pulse until the mixture reaches your desired jam consistency.
3. Spoon the raw apple jam into jars and refrigerate for at least 2 hours before serving.

C. Blender Apple Jam for Busy Days

Ingredients:

1. 4 cups finely chopped mixed apples (Fuji, Pink Lady)
2. 1/2 cup honey or agave nectar
3. 1 lemon (juiced)
4. 1 teaspoon vanilla extract

Instructions:

1. Place chopped apples, honey or agave nectar, lemon juice, and vanilla extract in a blender.
2. Blend until smooth.
3. Pour the mixture into jars and refrigerate for at least 2 hours before using.

These no-cook apple jam recipes offer a quick and convenient way to enjoy the delicious taste of homemade jam without the need for stovetop cooking. Perfect for those busy days or when you're looking for a simple and fresh jam option.

Chapter (13) Apple Jam Cocktails and Mocktails

A. Apple Jam Whiskey Sour
Ingredients:

- 2 oz whiskey
- 1 oz fresh lemon juice
- 1 tablespoon apple jam (Classic Apple Jam or preferred variation)
- Ice cubes
- Apple slices for garnish

Instructions:

1. In a shaker, combine whiskey, fresh lemon juice, and apple jam.
2. Add ice cubes and shake well.
3. Strain the mixture into a glass filled with ice.
4. Garnish with apple slices.
5. Enjoy your Apple Jam Whiskey Sour!

B. Sparkling Apple Jam Lemonade
Ingredients:

- 1 cup sparkling water
- 1/2 cup fresh lemonade
- 2 tablespoons apple jam (any variation)
- Ice cubes
- Lemon slices for garnish

Instructions:

- In a glass, combine sparkling water, fresh lemonade, and apple

jam.
- Stir well until the jam is dissolved.
- Add ice cubes and garnish with lemon slices.
- Refresh yourself with the Sparkling Apple Jam Lemonade!

C. Apple Jam Bellini for Celebrations
Ingredients:

- 2 oz apple brandy (Calvados)
- 1 tablespoon apple jam (any variation)
- Sparkling wine or Prosecco
- Apple slices for garnish

Instructions:

1. In a champagne flute, combine apple brandy and apple jam.
2. Stir well to mix.
3. Top up with sparkling wine or Prosecco.
4. Garnish with apple slices.
5. Raise a toast with the Apple Jam Bellini for your celebrations!

These delightful Apple Jam Cocktails and Mocktails add a unique twist to your beverage repertoire. Whether you're in the mood for a sophisticated Apple Jam Whiskey Sour, a refreshing Sparkling Apple Jam Lemonade, or a celebratory Apple Jam Bellini, these recipes offer a flavorful and enjoyable way to incorporate apple jam into your drink experiences.

Chapter (14) Apple Jam-Inspired Desserts

A. Apple Jam Thumbprint Cookies
Ingredients:

- 1 cup unsalted butter, softened
- 1/2 cup granulated sugar
- 2 large egg yolks
- 2 teaspoons vanilla extract
- 2 cups all-purpose flour
- 1/2 teaspoon salt
- Apple jam (any variation)

Instructions:

1. Preheat the oven to 350°F (175°C) and line a baking sheet with parchment paper.
2. In a large bowl, cream together butter and sugar until light and fluffy.
3. Beat in egg yolks and vanilla extract.
4. In a separate bowl, whisk together flour and salt.
5. Gradually add the dry ingredients to the wet ingredients, mixing until just combined.
6. Roll the dough into small balls and place them on the prepared baking sheet.
7. Make an indentation in the center of each cookie using your thumb or the back of a spoon.
8. Fill each indentation with a small spoonful of apple jam.
9. Bake for 12-15 minutes or until the edges are lightly golden.
10. Allow the cookies to cool before serving.

B. Apple Jam Cheesecake Bars
Ingredients:

- 2 cups graham cracker crumbs
- 1/2 cup unsalted butter, melted
- 16 oz cream cheese, softened
- 1 cup granulated sugar
- 1 teaspoon vanilla extract
- 3 large eggs
- 1 cup apple jam (any variation)

Instructions:

1. Preheat the oven to 325°F (160°C) and line a baking pan with parchment paper.
2. In a bowl, combine graham cracker crumbs and melted butter. Press into the bottom of the prepared pan to form the crust.
3. In a large mixing bowl, beat cream cheese, sugar, and vanilla extract until smooth.
4. Add eggs one at a time, beating well after each addition.
5. Pour the cream cheese mixture over the crust.
6. Drop spoonfuls of apple jam over the cream cheese layer and swirl with a knife.
7. Bake for 45-50 minutes or until the center is set.
8. Allow to cool before refrigerating for a few hours or overnight.
9. Cut into bars and serve.

C. Apple Jam Ice Cream Sundae

Ingredients:

- Vanilla ice cream
- Apple jam (any variation)
- Caramel sauce
- Chopped nuts (optional)
- Whipped cream
- Maraschino cherry for garnish

Instructions:

1. Scoop vanilla ice cream into a serving bowl.
2. Warm the apple jam slightly and drizzle it over the ice cream.
3. Add a generous drizzle of caramel sauce.
4. Sprinkle chopped nuts if desired.
5. Top with whipped cream and garnish with a maraschino cherry.
6. Indulge in the delightful Apple Jam Ice Cream Sundae.

These Apple Jam-Inspired Desserts are sure to satisfy your sweet tooth. Whether you're enjoying the fruity goodness of Apple Jam Thumbprint Cookies, the rich and creamy Apple Jam Cheesecake Bars, or the indulgent Apple Jam Ice Cream Sundae, these desserts are perfect for treating yourself and your loved ones.

Chapter (15) Homestead Orchard Tales

A. Visiting Local Orchards for Apple Picking
Story:

Embark on a journey to your local orchards during the crisp autumn days. The air is filled with the sweet scent of ripe apples, and the orchard is a patchwork of vibrant reds and golds. Families, friends, and even solo adventurers gather to partake in the age-old tradition of apple picking. The rustling leaves, the laughter of children, and the joy of reaching for the perfect apple create an unforgettable experience. Handpick a variety of apples to use in your homemade jams, connecting with the land and savoring the fruits of the season.

B. Preserving Family Traditions with Apple Jam
Story:

In the heart of the homestead, generations come together to preserve a cherished family tradition: making apple jam. Grandparents pass down their time-honored recipes, sharing stories of their own childhood kitchen adventures. The aroma of simmering apples and the warmth of shared memories fill the kitchen. As each jar is filled, sealed, and labeled with love, the family bonds over the simple joy of creating something meaningful. The apple jam becomes not just a delicious treat but a tangible link to the past, preserving family history one jar at a time.

C. Community Apple Jam-Making Events
Story:

In the spirit of community and sharing, the town organizes an annual Apple Jam-Making event. The local orchard generously donates bushels of apples, and the entire community gathers at a central location. Long tables are set up with chopping stations, sugar and spice stations, and rows of boiling pots. Neighbors, young and old, come together, peeling, chopping, and stirring in unison. Laughter fills the air as everyone contributes to the collective effort of making apple jam for the community. The event not only yields jars of delicious jam but fosters a sense of togetherness and shared accomplishment that lasts far beyond the day.

These Homestead Orchard Tales capture the essence of the apple-picking season, the importance of preserving family traditions through homemade jams, and the sense of community that flourishes during shared events. Whether you're savoring the harvest, creating lasting memories with loved ones, or uniting with your community over a bubbling pot of apple jam, these tales celebrate the simple joys found in the heart of the orchard.

Chapter (16) DIY Apple Jam Wedding Favors

A. Crafting Personalized Jam Jar Labels
  Instructions:

1. Choose a design that complements your wedding theme and colors.
2. Create a personalized label with the couple's names, wedding date, and a heartfelt message.
3. Include the jam flavor and a short description for a touch of elegance.
4. Print the labels on adhesive paper or cardstock.
5. Cut out each label and affix it to the jam jars.

B. Tips for Mass Production of Wedding Favors
Tips:

1. Plan ahead and start early to avoid last-minute stress.
2. Break the process into manageable tasks, such as chopping apples or labeling, and tackle them gradually.
3. Enlist the help of family and friends for a fun and collaborative experience.
4. Create an assembly line with designated roles to streamline the production.
5. Allocate a specific timeframe for the production process, ensuring you have enough time for other wedding preparations.

C. Unique Apple Jam Flavor Combinations for Weddings
  Romantic Rose Apple Jam:

Use fragrant roses to infuse a delicate floral note into the jam. Perfect for a romantic wedding setting.

Lavender and Honey Apple Jam:

Combine lavender flowers and honey for a soothing and aromatic jam. Ideal for a rustic or garden-themed wedding.

Champagne-Infused Apple Jam:

Add a touch of luxury with a hint of champagne, creating an elegant flavor profile for a sophisticated wedding.

Citrus Burst Apple Jam:

Zest up your jam with citrus fruits like oranges and lemons for a refreshing and lively twist, fitting for a summer wedding.

Berry Bliss Apple Jam:

Mix in a variety of berries like strawberries, blueberries, and raspberries for a burst of color and sweetness, perfect for a vibrant wedding celebration.

Exotic Spiced Apple Jam:

Infuse warm spices such as cinnamon, cloves, and nutmeg for an exotic and cozy flavor, suitable for fall or winter weddings.

Create a memorable and personal touch for your wedding with these DIY Apple Jam Wedding Favors. From crafting personalized labels to efficiently mass-producing the favors, and exploring unique flavor combinations, these tips and ideas will make your wedding favors both delicious and unforgettable.

Chapter (16) Apple Jam and Cheese Pairing Guide

A. Creating a Perfect Cheese Board with Apple Jam

Instructions:

Cheese Selection:

Choose a variety of cheeses, including soft, semi-soft, and hard cheeses. Examples include brie, gouda, cheddar, and blue cheese.

Crackers and Bread:

Include a selection of crackers, baguette slices, and breadsticks to complement the cheeses.

Fresh and Dried Fruits:

Add fresh apple slices, grapes, or figs for a burst of sweetness. Dried fruits like apricots or cranberries also work well.

Nuts:

Include a mix of nuts such as almonds, walnuts, or pecans for added texture.

Charcuterie (Optional):

Add cured meats like prosciutto or salami to enhance the savory elements.

Apple Jam:

Place a jar of your favorite apple jam on the board for a delightful sweet and tangy contrast.

B. Pairing Apple Jam with Different Cheese Varieties

Brie and Vanilla Bean Apple Jam:

Creamy brie pairs beautifully with the subtle sweetness of vanilla bean apple jam.

Gouda and Maple-Pecan Apple Jam:

The nuttiness of gouda complements the rich flavors of maple-pecan apple jam.

Cheddar and Apple-Rosemary Jam:

Sharp cheddar contrasts well with the savory notes of apple-rosemary jam.

Blue Cheese and Bourbon-Infused Apple Jam:

The bold and tangy blue cheese pairs excellently with the complex flavors of bourbon-infused apple jam.

Goat Cheese and Honey-Apple Jam:

The creamy texture of goat cheese is enhanced by the sweet and floral notes of honey-apple jam.

C. Hosting a Cheese and Jam Tasting Party

Tips:

Variety is Key:

Offer a diverse selection of cheeses, jams, and accompaniments to cater to different preferences.

Tasting Cards:

Create tasting cards describing each cheese and jam pairing. Include flavor notes and suggested pairings.

Palette Cleansers:

Provide water and plain crackers as palate cleansers between tastings.

Interactive Experience:

Encourage guests to mix and match different cheeses and jams to discover their favorite combinations.

Decor and Presentation:

Arrange the cheese board aesthetically with attention to colors, shapes, and textures. Consider using slate boards or wooden platters for an elegant presentation.

Elevate your culinary experience with this Apple Jam and Cheese Pairing Guide. Whether you're creating a perfect cheese board, exploring diverse pairings, or hosting a cheese and jam tasting party, these ideas will delight your taste buds and impress your guests with a symphony of flavors.

Chapter (17) Apple Jam for Wellness

A. Incorporating Apple Jam into Breakfast Bowls
Recipe: Apple Jam Breakfast Bowl
Ingredients:

- Greek yogurt or your favorite plant-based yogurt
- Granola
- Fresh fruits (sliced apples, berries, banana)
- Nuts and seeds (almonds, chia seeds)
- Drizzle of apple jam (any variation)

Instructions:

1. In a bowl, layer Greek yogurt.
2. Top with granola for crunch and texture.
3. Add a variety of fresh fruits and a sprinkle of nuts and seeds.
4. Finish with a drizzle of apple jam for a sweet and flavorful touch.
5. Mix well before enjoying your nutritious and delicious Apple Jam Breakfast Bowl.

B. Apple Jam Infused Herbal Teas
Recipe: Apple Jam Herbal Tea Infusion
Ingredients:

- 1 herbal tea bag (such as chamomile or peppermint)
- 1 tablespoon apple jam (Classic Apple Jam or preferred variation)
- Hot water

Instructions:

1. Place the herbal tea bag in a cup.

2. Add hot water and let it steep according to the tea's instructions.
3. Stir in a tablespoon of apple jam until fully dissolved.
4. Remove the tea bag and enjoy your soothing Apple Jam Infused Herbal Tea.

C. Apple Jam as a Flavorful Yogurt Topping
Instructions:

1. Spoon your favorite yogurt (Greek, regular, or plant-based) into a bowl.
2. Swirl in a generous spoonful of apple jam for natural sweetness and flavor.
3. Top with additional toppings like granola, nuts, or fresh fruit for added texture.
4. Mix well and savor the delightful combination of creamy yogurt and sweet apple jam.

Incorporating apple jam into your daily routine adds a touch of sweetness and flavor while boosting your wellness. Whether enjoyed in a nutritious breakfast bowl, infused into herbal teas, or used as a flavorful yogurt topping, these ideas make wellness a delightful and delicious experience.

Chapter (18) Preserving Memories: Scrapbooking with Apple Jam Labels

A. Creative Ways to Document Your Jam-Making Journey

Ideas:

Photo Collage:

Create a visual journey of your jam-making process, from selecting apples to the final jars. Include candid shots and close-ups of the ingredients and equipment.

Recipe Cards:

Design personalized recipe cards with details about each apple jam variation. Include notes on flavor profiles, occasions, and any special memories associated with each recipe.

Pressed Apple Prints:

Preserve slices of apples used in your jam by pressing them onto pages. This adds a sensory element to your scrapbook.

Handwritten Notes:

Add handwritten notes capturing your thoughts, feelings, and experiences throughout the jam-making adventure. These personal touches create a connection to the memories.

B. Turning Jam Labels into Art

Steps:

Label Collection:

Collect the labels from your apple jam jars. Gently remove them to keep them intact.

Collage Creation:

Arrange the labels on a canvas or thick paper in a visually appealing collage. Overlap them, mix sizes, and experiment with different orientations.

Mod Podge Sealing:

Use Mod Podge to seal the labels onto the canvas. Apply a thin layer over the labels, ensuring they adhere securely.

Additional Elements:

Enhance the collage with additional elements like pressed flowers, fabric scraps, or small illustrations related to the apple jam theme.

C. Making a Family Recipe Book with Apple Jam Stories
Steps:
Gather Family Recipes:
Collect recipes passed down through generations, including apple jam variations. Ask family members to share their favorites.

Incorporate Jam Stories:
Integrate stories and anecdotes related to the apple jam-making process. Share memories, occasions, and the joy of creating homemade jam.

Design and Layout:
Use a scrapbooking approach to design pages. Include space for recipes, photos, and handwritten notes. Decorate with apple-themed embellishments.

Personalize Each Page:
Personalize each page with the contributor's name, a photo, or a small illustration. This creates a unique and heartfelt family recipe book.

Preserve the memories of your jam-making journey with creativity and personal touches. Whether through a visual scrapbook capturing the process, turning labels into art, or creating a family recipe book with stories, these ideas ensure that every jar of apple jam is not just a delicious treat but a cherished memory.

Chapter (19) Apple Jam and Cultural Festivals

A. Celebrating Apple Harvest Festivals
Ideas:

Apple Jam Tasting Booth:

Set up a booth at the festival where attendees can sample various apple jam flavors. Provide small tasting spoons and engage visitors in conversations about the unique qualities of each jam.

Jam-Making Demonstrations:

Host live demonstrations showcasing the art of making apple jam. Share tips, techniques, and the cultural significance of preserving fruits through jams.

Apple Jam Cooking Contests:

Organize friendly cooking competitions where participants create their own apple jam recipes. Judges can evaluate based on taste, creativity, and cultural inspiration.

Cultural Performances:

Integrate cultural performances, music, and dances into the festival. Create a vibrant atmosphere that celebrates both the harvest season and the diverse cultural backgrounds of attendees.

B. Sharing Apple Jam at Cultural Events
Suggestions:

Potluck Cultural Dinners:

Encourage attendees to bring dishes that represent their cultural backgrounds. Share apple jam as a versatile condiment that complements various cuisines.

Cultural Exchange Events:

Host events where people can share their culinary traditions. Have a section dedicated to apple jam, allowing attendees to taste and exchange recipes.

Workshops on Cultural Preserving:

Conduct workshops focusing on the cultural aspects of preserving fruits, including the significance of apple jam in various traditions.

Cultural Jam Swap:

Organize a jam swap where attendees bring homemade jams representing their cultural heritage. This fosters a sense of community and appreciation for diverse flavors.

C. Preserving Cultural Heritage through Apple Jam

Steps:

Cultural-Inspired Jam Recipes:

Develop apple jam recipes inspired by various cultures. Consider using spices, fruits, or techniques that reflect the culinary traditions of different regions.

Storytelling Labels:

Create labels for your apple jam jars that include stories or anecdotes about the cultural inspiration behind each flavor. Share the significance of the ingredients and the cultural context.

Collaborative Cultural Jams:

Collaborate with individuals from diverse cultural backgrounds to create unique apple jam blends. This collaborative effort celebrates cultural diversity and promotes understanding through shared culinary experiences.

Cultural Awareness Events:

Organize events that raise awareness about the importance of preserving cultural heritage through food. Engage in discussions, showcase traditional recipes, and highlight the role of apple jam in cultural kitchens.

By celebrating apple jam at cultural festivals, sharing it at events, and preserving cultural heritage through unique recipes, you can create connections, foster appreciation for diversity, and showcase the rich tapestry of culinary traditions. These initiatives bring people together through the shared joy of food and cultural expression.

Chapter (20) Vegan Apple Jam Options

A. Plant-Based Sweeteners for Vegan Jam

Options:

Maple Syrup:

Replace traditional sugar with pure maple syrup for a rich and natural sweetness.

Agave Nectar:

Agave nectar provides a sweet and mild flavor, making it an excellent alternative to traditional sweeteners.

Coconut Sugar:

Coconut sugar offers a caramel-like sweetness, adding depth to your vegan apple jam.

Date Paste:

Blend soaked dates into a paste to naturally sweeten your jam. Dates also contribute a delightful fruity flavor.

B. Vegan Apple Jam Recipes without Pectin
Recipe: Simple Vegan Apple Jam
Ingredients:

- 6 cups apples, peeled, cored, and chopped
- 1 cup plant-based sweetener (maple syrup, agave nectar, or coconut sugar)
- 1 lemon, juiced
- 1 teaspoon ground cinnamon

Instructions:

1. In a large pot, combine chopped apples, plant-based sweetener, lemon juice, and cinnamon.
2. Bring the mixture to a boil over medium heat.
3. Reduce heat to low and simmer, stirring occasionally, until the apples break down and the jam thickens (about 30-40 minutes).
4. Mash any remaining large pieces of apple with a fork or potato masher.
5. Allow the jam to cool before transferring it to sterilized jars.
6. Refrigerate for up to two weeks or follow proper canning procedures for longer shelf life.

C. Vegan-Friendly Apple Jam-Filled Pastries
Recipe: Vegan Apple Jam Turnovers
Ingredients:

- Vegan puff pastry sheets
- Vegan apple jam (any variation)
- Plant-based milk for brushing
- Powdered sugar for dusting

Instructions:

1. Preheat the oven according to the puff pastry package instructions.
2. Roll out the puff pastry sheets and cut them into squares.
3. Spoon a small amount of vegan apple jam into the center of each square.
4. Fold the pastry over the jam, creating triangles. Seal the edges with a fork.
5. Place the turnovers on a lined baking sheet.
6. Brush the tops with plant-based milk for a golden finish.
7. Bake according to the puff pastry package instructions, usually around 15-20 minutes.
8. Once cooled, dust the turnovers with powdered sugar before serving.

These vegan apple jam options showcase the versatility of plant-based sweeteners, provide a pectin-free jam recipe, and offer a delightful vegan-friendly pastry filled with the goodness of homemade apple jam. Enjoy the delicious flavors without compromising your vegan lifestyle.

Chapter (21) Festive Holiday Extravaganza: Spiced Apple Jam Gift Collection

A. Crafting Seasonal Apple Jam Gift Sets

Ideas:

Personalized Jar Labels:

Create festive and personalized labels for your apple jam jars. Include holiday-themed designs, messages, or even customize them with recipients' names for a thoughtful touch.

Gift Basket Creations:

Build gift baskets with an assortment of your favorite apple jam variations. Include complementary items like crackers, cheeses, and a cozy tea blend for a complete holiday experience.

DIY Packaging:

Craft your own packaging with holiday-themed materials. Consider using festive fabric, ribbons, or even repurposing old holiday cards for a sustainable and charming touch.

Customized Recipe Cards:

Include recipe cards showcasing creative ways to use your spiced apple jam. Inspire recipients with ideas for festive desserts, savory dishes, or even holiday cocktails.

B. Holiday Spice Blend Apple Jam for Winter Warmth

Recipe: Holiday Spice Blend Apple Jam

Ingredients:

- 6 cups apples, peeled, cored, and diced
- 2 cups granulated sugar
- 1 cup brown sugar
- 1 cup apple cider
- 1 tablespoon ground cinnamon

- 1 teaspoon ground nutmeg
- 1/2 teaspoon ground cloves
- 1/2 teaspoon ground allspice
- 1/4 teaspoon salt
- Zest and juice of one orange

Instructions:

1. In a large pot, combine apples, sugars, apple cider, cinnamon, nutmeg, cloves, allspice, salt, orange zest, and orange juice.
2. Bring the mixture to a boil over medium heat, stirring occasionally.
3. Reduce the heat to low and simmer for 45-60 minutes or until the jam thickens, and the apples are soft.
4. Mash any remaining large pieces of apple with a fork or potato masher.
5. Allow the jam to cool before transferring it to sterilized jars.
6. Seal the jars and refrigerate for up to two weeks or follow proper canning procedures for a longer shelf life.

**C. Cranberry-Orange Apple Jam for a Festive Citrus Twist
Recipe: Cranberry-Orange Apple Jam
Ingredients:**

- 4 cups apples, peeled, cored, and chopped
- 2 cups cranberries, fresh or frozen
- 2 cups granulated sugar
- Zest and juice of two oranges
- 1 teaspoon vanilla extract

Instructions:

1. In a saucepan, combine apples, cranberries, sugar, orange zest, and orange juice.
2. Bring the mixture to a boil, then reduce heat and simmer until the fruit is soft and the jam thickens (about 30 minutes).
3. Stir in vanilla extract and continue to simmer for an additional 5 minutes.
4. Allow the jam to cool before transferring it to sterilized jars.
5. Seal the jars and refrigerate for up to two weeks or follow proper canning procedures for a longer shelf life.

Transform your holiday season into a festive extravaganza with a Spiced Apple Jam Gift Collection. Craft personalized gift sets, create a warm and aromatic Holiday Spice Blend Apple Jam, and indulge in a Festive Citrus Twist with Cranberry-Orange Apple Jam. These recipes and gift ideas will make your holidays extra special and delight your loved ones with the warmth of homemade goodness.

Chapter (22) Culinary Adventures with Apple Jam: Cooking Classes and Workshops

A. Hosting Apple Jam-Making Classes
Ideas:
Seasonal Themes:
Tailor your classes to the seasons, such as hosting "Fall Harvest Apple Jam-Making" or "Springtime Blossom-inspired Jams."
Virtual Classes:
Reach a wider audience by hosting virtual apple jam-making classes. Provide participants with ingredient lists in advance for an interactive online experience.
Hands-On Experience:
Offer participants a hands-on experience by providing all the necessary ingredients and equipment. Guide them through the jam-making process step-by step.
Customized Packages:
Create customized class packages for different skill levels, from beginner to advanced. Include take-home materials like recipe cards and jar labels.

B. Collaborating with Local Chefs for Special Workshops
Collaborative Ideas:
Chef-Led Workshops:
Collaborate with local chefs to conduct special apple jam-making workshops. Introduce unique flavor combinations and innovative culinary techniques.
Farm-to-Table Experiences:

Partner with local farms to source fresh, seasonal ingredients. Host workshops that showcase the journey from orchard to kitchen, emphasizing the importance of locally sourced produce.

Pairing Sessions:

Collaborate with chefs to create pairing sessions that combine apple jams with local cheeses, bread, or even craft beverages. Elevate the workshop into a multisensory culinary experience.

Recipe Development:

Work with chefs to develop exclusive apple jam recipes that highlight their culinary expertise. These recipes can then be shared with workshop participants.

C. Creating a Community of Apple Jam Enthusiasts

Community-Building Initiatives:

Online Forums:

Establish online forums or social media groups where participants from your classes and workshops can share their experiences, exchange tips, and ask questions.

Jam-Making Challenges:

Organize friendly jam-making challenges within the community. Encourage participants to experiment with different flavors and share their creations.

Local Meetups:

Host local meetups or events where members of the apple jam community can gather, share their homemade jams, and discuss their culinary adventures.

Collaborative Projects:

Initiate collaborative projects, such as creating a community recipe book featuring diverse apple jam recipes from members. This fosters a sense of camaraderie and shared creativity.

Embark on culinary adventures with apple jam by hosting engaging and educational classes and workshops. Whether you're guiding participants through the jam-making process, collaborating with local chefs for special events, or building a community of apple jam enthusiasts, these initiatives create a vibrant and inclusive space for culinary exploration and shared passion.

Chapter (23) The Science of Jam: Understanding Pectin and Gel Points

A. Exploring the Chemistry Behind Apple Jam

Topics:

Pectin and Fruit Preservation:

Delve into the role of pectin in fruit preservation and how it contributes to the gel-like consistency of jams. Understand how different fruits, including apples, contain varying levels of natural pectin.

Chemical Reactions in Jam-Making:

Explore the chemical reactions that occur during the jam-making process. Understand how heat, sugar, and acidity work together to create the desired texture and preserve the fruit.

Impact of Apple Varieties:

Investigate how the choice of apple varieties influences the pectin content and overall texture of the jam. Learn which apples are high in pectin and suitable for achieving a well-set jam.

Pectin Alternatives:

Discuss alternatives to traditional pectin, such as natural sources like citrus peels or techniques like using apple cores and seeds. Explore how these alternatives affect the gelling process.

B. Tips for Achieving the Perfect Gel Point

Guidance:

Testing Gel Point:

Understand the importance of reaching the gel point for the desired jam consistency. Learn how to perform the plate or spoon test to determine when your jam has reached the optimal thickness.

Temperature Control:

Explore the impact of temperature on the gel point. Gain insights into maintaining consistent heat throughout the cooking process to achieve the perfect gel without overcooking.

Acidity Balance:

Learn about the role of acidity in achieving the gel point. Discover how balancing acidity with sugar and the natural acidity of fruits contributes to a stable gel.

Proper Stirring Techniques:

Master the art of stirring during the cooking process. Understand how consistent stirring prevents uneven gel distribution and promotes a smooth, well-set jam.

C. Troubleshooting Common Pectin-related Issues

Common Issues and Solutions:

Jam that Doesn't Set:

Identify reasons why jams may not set properly and explore troubleshooting steps. Factors such as incorrect pectin levels, insufficient cooking time, or improper temperature control can impact setting.

Excessive Setting or Grainy Texture:

Understand why jams may become overly set or develop a grainy texture. Explore adjustments to pectin levels, sugar content, or cooking times to achieve the desired consistency.

Natural Pectin Extraction Techniques:

Discuss techniques for naturally extracting pectin from fruit peels, cores, and seeds. Learn how to incorporate these elements into your jam-making process to enhance natural gelling.

Balancing Flavors with Pectin Usage:

Gain insights into balancing the use of commercial pectin with the natural flavors of fruits. Understand how to achieve a harmonious blend that preserves the essence of the ingredients.

Unlock the secrets of the science behind apple jam-making, from the chemistry of pectin to achieving the perfect gel point. With a deeper understanding of the role of pectin, temperature control, and troubleshooting common issues, you'll elevate your jam-making skills and produce consistently delightful results.

❖ Conclusion

A. Celebrating the Joy of Homemade Apple Jam

Embarking on the journey of creating homemade apple jam is not just a culinary experience; it's a celebration of flavors, traditions, and the joy that comes from crafting something delicious with your own hands. As you savor the fruits of your labor, relish in the memories of apple-picking adventures, shared moments in the kitchen, and the delightful aromas that fill your home. Each jar of apple jam is a testament to your creativity and dedication to preserving the essence of this beloved fruit.

B. Share Your Creations and Connect with Fellow Jam Enthusiasts

Your apple jam creations are a labor of love, and what better way to enhance the experience than by sharing it with others? Whether gifting a jar to a friend, hosting a tasting party, or participating in community events, your homemade apple jam becomes a delightful gift that spreads joy. Connect with fellow jam enthusiasts, exchange recipes, and celebrate the diverse and wonderful world of homemade preserves.

As you continue your apple jam-making journey, remember that each batch tells a story, and each jar holds the potential to create lasting memories. Cherish the tradition, revel in the flavors, and let the joy of homemade apple jam bring sweetness to your life and the lives of those you share it with.